DECIDE YOUR DESTINY

You Can Be What You Want To Be

MAXIM CASTELINO

INDIA · SINGAPORE · MALAYSIA

Table of Contents

Chapter 9: Father of Spirits

Chapter 10: The Final Victory

Preface

We are all born here on earth not knowing why we are here, where we came from, and where we are going. All of our life principles have come partly from our parents, our elders, and our religious leaders. We never questioned their authenticity because we love and honor them. It's just like going to a doctor, getting the prescribed medicines, and consuming them. It is possible that the doctor may have prescribed the wrong medicine due to a wrong diagnosis. We only realize this when we discover that the sickness has not been healed, and moreover, the wrong medicines have caused another complication within the body. Had we sought a second opinion from another doctor, we may not have had to suffer the effects of the wrong medicine. Similarly, it is possible that the life principles we have imbibed from those who nurtured us may not be accurate and could be detrimental to our lives. So, there is a need to discover if there are better life principles than the ones we have been raised with.

We all have ambitions and goals of our own to live a better life. We strive to reach our goals through means such as education, jobs, businesses, investments, advertisements, campaigns, and the like. As we come to maturity, we get married, have children, and want to live a comfortable life. Sometimes things may not go as expected, and we end up living a mixed life with both sorrows and happiness. Whether we like it or not, one fine day, we pass away from this earth. Is that all there is to life, or is there something more? We should know if there is an afterlife, and if there is, we should prepare for that life even right now.

Suppose you found the answers to all your life questions, and if those answers are found to be contrary to the beliefs of your parents, elders, religious leaders, or even your government, they will either try to control you, intimidate you, influence you, or do their best to make you not believe in your convictions. We have all been created by God and not by our parents. Our parents were only the means by which

God brought us into this world. In the eyes of God, we are all created equal, and we have all been given our individual rights to seek God and to know the Truth. We must realize this dilemma and ask ourselves a question, "How long will I live in my state of ignorance and falsehood?"

Sometimes our own die-hard beliefs will not let us accept and receive the Truth. This could be our pride or prejudice. Because of this, there is a tendency to say, "I was born this way, I will die this way" or "I am proud to be such and such." In such times, we do not realize the kind of damage we cause to ourselves by saying so. If we are true to ourselves, we must fight ignorance, deception, and lies, and we must refuse anyone from influencing us to remain in the state where we are. Due to the die-hard attitudes of some people, they remain poor and sorrowful throughout their lives.

If the product you purchased has a fault, you would read the manual provided by the manufacturer. It is unwise to seek information about the product from your best friend. It is possible that your best friend has never used that product or may only know something about it. To gain a holistic understanding of the product, it is always better to read the manual provided by the manufacturer. Since God is the one who created us, we must refer to God's manual when it comes to our life issues. It is unwise to obtain information about God from our parents or anyone else. God's manual contains the truth, and the truth is found in the pages of the Bible. When you know the truth and apply it in your life, you will be considered a wise person.

The fear of the Lord is the beginning of wisdom. We must fear God because He is almighty, all-knowing, and omnipresent. In other words, He is omnipotent, omniscient, and omnipresent. We should also fear God because He alone can judge us and condemn us if we are found to have transgressed His commandments. Today, fear is considered to be an unhealthy attitude. However, there are many people who say that because their dad was strict and because their schoolteachers were strict, they were able to reach a good position in life. Without them, we would have been undisciplined people and could not have achieved much.

Most of us have been programmed to believe that we must do good to appease God, and if our good deeds outweigh our bad deeds, somehow we will be saved. This is a man-made concept, and the Bible does not support it. According to the Bible, mankind is incapable of keeping God's commandments. Therefore, God decided to incarnate Himself as a human being, calling Himself Jesus and paid the penalty for our sins on the cross of Calvary. The blood He shed on the cross is the means by which our sins are forgiven. As we believe in this fact and make Jesus Christ our Lord and Savior, the Holy Spirit begins to dwell within us through whom we will be saved.

All of us at one time or another have encountered the conflict that goes on within us. While we decide to live a good life, there are forces within us that do not allow us to do so. That is because we have two lives within us: the life of the spirit and the life of the flesh. Our spirit always desires to live by God's principles while our flesh desires the things of this world. For this reason, God sent His Holy Spirit to live within us so we can overcome the desires of our flesh and abide by the desires of our spirit. As we continue to live by our spirit, we will eventually be transformed to embody godly character, which will be manifested in our daily lives. This godly character will enable us to bless others and change this world. This is our destiny in this world, besides the eternal destiny that God has freely offered to us to live in heaven with Him.

CHAPTER 1

Understanding the Fundamentals

THE BIBLE

Many people argue if the Bible is historically true or scientifically true. Even though the Bible does contain history, poetry, and prophecies, it was never meant to be read from a historical or scientific perspective. It was meant to be read from a spiritual perspective. It was meant to learn about God and his character. It was also meant to learn about our shortcomings and how we can overcome them.

The Bible consists of 66 books, of which the first 39 belong to the Old Testament and the other 27 belong to the New Testament. The Old Testament was written prior to the advent of Jesus, while the New Testament was written after the ascension of Jesus to heaven. The Old Testament is primarily speaking to the Jews, while the New Testament is speaking to Christians.

The first five books of the Old Testament are called the Pentateuch. It contains the laws given by God to Moses. The rest of the Old Testament contains history, poetry, and prophecies. The first four books of the New Testament are called the Gospel. They describe the life and ministry of Jesus Christ. The rest of the New Testament contains history, epistles, and prophecy. The last book of the New Testament is called Revelation, which is a prophetic book explaining the events that would take place before the return of Jesus Christ to establish his kingdom on earth. The

Bible can also be referred to as the Word of God. Studying the Word of God can also be called meditating on the Word of God.

GOD

Many people have an aversion to God because of how religious people live. There are also other reasons why they do not believe in God. For example, when godly principles go against their lifestyle or when they do not get answers to life's trivial questions, such as when people die of starvation, when children die in wars, or when women are raped and illegitimate children are born. The reason they do not receive answers to all these questions is because they want to remain ignorant.

Scientific laws were not given to the scientists on a silver spoon. It was discovered after many efforts were put in throughout their entire lives. Similarly, God does not answer any spiritual question unless the person invests time in seeking the answer from the Bible. God is understood by what he has said in the Bible. When we read the Bible, we understand God. Even though God lives in heaven, he has chosen to live in our hearts, if we are willing. He has promised to teach us everything about himself and what he desires from us.

> *Before the mountains were brought forth, or ever thou hadst formed the earth and the world, Even from everlasting to everlasting, thou art God.*
>
> *– Psa. 90:2*

God is an eternal being who lives in eternity. He does not have a beginning or end. He is the creator of all things and all beings. He loves mankind so much that he wants to give us a position higher than that of angels. It's not just any position. He wants to adopt us as his own children. He wants to transform us into his own image and his own likeness. He wants us all to have the character of Christ in us. God lives in the third heaven.

For there are three that bear record in heaven, the Father, the Word, and the Holy Ghost: and these three are one.

– 1 John 5:7

God is a triune being, which means God lives in three persons but is yet one in being. They are the Father, the Son, and the Holy Spirit. The Father legislates the laws, the Son executes the laws, and the Holy Spirit is the means by which the law is executed. The Son is a term given to Jesus Christ, who is God himself incarnated as human. God demonstrated his love to mankind through Jesus Christ by means of healing the sick, setting people free from demonic oppression, raising dead people to life, and finally by offering himself as a sacrifice on the cross of Calvary. The Holy Spirit is the spirit of God and of Jesus Christ who lives in those who have made Jesus Christ the Lord of their lives.

SATAN

How art thou fallen from heaven, O Lucifer, son of the morning! how art thou cut down to the ground, which didst weaken the nations!

– Isa. 14:12

Satan was originally known as Lucifer when he was created as an angelic being and was given the position of cherubim in heaven. Generally, a cherub guards the throne of God. However, because of the beauty and wisdom that God had given Lucifer, he became proud and decided to make his own throne and act like God. As he was thinking about it, God deposed him from his position as cherubim, cast him down to the earth, and made him known as Satan. As Satan fell, he took with him one-third of the heavenly angels, and they came to be known as demons. He succeeded in deceiving Eve, took the authority that God had given to Adam, and set up his throne in second heaven.

LIGHT AND DARKNESS

The light of the body is the eye: if therefore thine eye be single, thy whole body shall be full of light. But if thine eye be evil, thy whole body shall be full of darkness. If therefore the light that is in thee be darkness, how great is that darkness!

– Mat. 6:22, 23

The Bible uses the word light to signify any person who has the Holy Spirit within him or her. It also implies the revelation of the Word of God. The word darkness signifies the devil and the demons. Darkness also implies having no revelation of the Word of God. Here, the scripture says that we must keep focusing on the Word of God and not to deviate from it for any reason. The moment we deviate from the Word of God, darkness will invade our life.

CHAPTER 2

The Creation of Man

THE FIRST HUMANS

And the Lord God commanded the man, saying, Of every tree of the garden thou mayest freely eat: but of the tree of the knowledge of good and evil, thou shalt not eat of it: for in the day that thou eatest thereof thou shalt surely die.

– Gen. 2:16-17

The Bible says that God had planned to create humans even before he laid the foundation of the earth. He had predestined them to live with him forever. When God created Adam, the first human being, Satan and his demons were already on the earth. When God placed Adam in the Garden of Eden, Satan had already occupied a tree in the middle of the garden called the Tree of the Knowledge of Good and Evil. God had told Adam not to eat the fruit of that tree, and if he did eat, he would die.

God also created Eve, the first woman, using one of the ribs from Adam and gave her to be Adam's wife. Both Adam and Eve were in perfect relationship with God. One fine day, Satan played a trick on Eve and deceived her into eating the forbidden fruit, and she gave it to Adam to eat as well. This broke the relationship of Adam and Eve with God. God cursed and banished them from entering the garden. This disconnection of their relationship with God was the fulfillment of God's warning to Adam that if he ate the forbidden fruit, he would die.

THE AUTHORITY OF MAN

So God created man in his own image, in the image of God created he him; male and female created he them. And God blessed them, and God said unto them, Be fruitful, and multiply, and replenish the earth, and subdue it: and have dominion over the fish of the sea, and over the fowl of the air, and over every living thing that moveth upon the earth.

– Gen. 1:27, 28

When God created Adam, he was created in God's image, and both Adam and Eve were given authority over all the living beings on the earth. They were blessed and commanded to multiply, replenish, and subdue the earth. They were given herbs and fruits to eat from the garden. However, when Adam and Eve fell into sin, their authority was stolen by Satan, and they were disconnected from God. From then on, they were enslaved by their sin, and Satan ruled over them.

THE ANATOMY OF MAN

And the Lord God formed man of the dust of the ground, and breathed into his nostrils the breath of life; and man became a living soul.

– Gen. 2:7

Just as God is a triune being, man is also a triune being. Man was created in the image of God. When God created Adam, he was made of clay, and God breathed into this clay to form man. The breath of God became the spirit of man, the clay became the body of man, and man became a living soul. It means man is comprised of the spirit, soul, and body. However, the real person of a man is the soul. The spirit and the body are only the influencing factors over his soul. While the spirit of man connects to God, the body of man connects to this world. Therefore, the spirit influences the soul on godly things while the body influences the soul on material things. The soul is the ultimate decision-maker. The soul decides whether to be influenced by the spirit or the body. The soul also has the discretion not to be influenced either by the spirit or the body but to make its own decisions based on intellect, conscience or emotions.

THE STATE OF THE SOUL

And unto Adam he said, Because thou hast hearkened unto the voice of thy wife, and hast eaten of the tree, of which I commanded thee, saying, Thou shalt not eat of it: cursed is the ground for thy sake; in sorrow shalt thou eat of it all the days of thy life; thorns also and thistles shall it bring forth to thee; and thou shalt eat the herb of the field; in the sweat of thy face shalt thou eat bread, till thou return unto the ground; for out of it wast thou taken: for dust thou art, and unto dust shalt thou return.

– Gen. 3:17-19

When Adam fell into sin, he lost his relationship with God. In other words, his spirit died. The death of the spirit indicates disconnection from God. Therefore, the spirit can no longer influence the soul on godly matters. The body, on the other hand, connects with the material world and experiences the five senses of sight, sound, smell, taste, and touch. Now that Adam and Eve had both received the curse from God, there was no way for them to live a righteous life. Because the spirit has died, the body takes a dominant role in influencing the soul. Based on the person's conscience, the soul decides whether to be influenced by the body or not. Each time the person decides to go against the conscience and indulges in the pleasures of the body, the conscience fades little by little. As long as the person listens to his conscience, he remains civilized. Every time he caters to the demands of his body, he becomes animalistic. So, every person has a dual nature of being a civilized person at certain times and being animalistic at other times.

AREAS OF TEMPTATION

And when the woman saw that the tree was good for food, and that it was pleasant to the eyes, and a tree to be desired to make one wise, she took of the fruit thereof, and did eat, and gave also unto her husband with her; and he did eat.

– Gen. 3:6

When Eve was tempted by the serpent, it was in three areas. She saw that the tree was good for food. So, the first area of temptation is physical need. Then she also saw that it was pleasant to the eyes. So, the second area of temptation is beauty. Then she also saw that the tree should be desired to make one wise. So, the third temptation is knowledge. This is not the knowledge of God, but of the world. When we seek knowledge outside of God's will, we are trying to be independent of God. Independence from God can be considered as pride.

Love not the world, neither the things that are in the world. If any man love the world, the love of the Father is not in him. For all that is in the world, the lust of the flesh, and the lust of the eyes, and the pride of life, is not of the Father, but is of the world.

– 1 John 2:15, 16

All temptations lead us toward this world. If we ever desire the things of this world, it means that we do not love God. The three areas of temptation in this world are physical needs (flesh), beauty, and pride.

But if our gospel be hid, it is hid to them that are lost: in whom the god of this world hath blinded the minds of them which believe not, lest the light of the glorious gospel of Christ, who is the image of God, should shine unto them.

– 2 Cor. 4:3, 4

Because we are prone to temptation and fall into sin, Satan has taken advantage of mankind and blinded their spiritual mind from knowing the truth.

SOUL AND EMOTIONS

If any man come to me, and hate not his father, and mother, and wife, and children, and brethren, and sisters, yea, and his own life also, he cannot be my disciple.

– Luk. 14:26

It is not just our body and conscience that influence our soul. Our emotions also influence our soul. As we are very much attached to our parents and siblings, they can always influence us to live according to their demands. We are also attached to our friends, customs, culture, language, society, and nation. Any of these can also influence us to live according to their demands. Unless we shed our emotions and decide to live according to God's demands, all of these influencing factors can draw us back from our spiritual progress. We must break free from any attachment to these external factors that hinder our spiritual growth.

THE CONCEPT OF FLESH

Now the works of the flesh are manifest, which are these; Adultery, fornication, uncleanness, lasciviousness, idolatry, witchcraft, hatred, variance, emulations, wrath, strife, seditions, heresies, envyings, murders, drunkenness, revellings, and such like: of the which I tell you before, as I have also told you in time past, that they which do such things shall not inherit the kingdom of God.

– Gal. 5:19-21

Whenever our soul gives in to the demands of our body to enjoy the pleasures of this world, our soul becomes normalized to such behavior. Therefore, the term "flesh" is used in the Bible to describe that part of the soul that has normalized bad behavior. Therefore, the character of a person is a combination of his conscience, emotions, and flesh. If we want to please God, our flesh acts as the primary enemy against us in pleasing God.

GOODNESS WITHOUT GOD

But we are all as an unclean thing, and all our righteousnesses are as filthy rags; and we all do fade as a leaf; and our iniquities, like the wind, have taken us away.

— Isa. 64:6

Because of the dual behavior in man, which is civilized and animalistic, there is always a conflict going on within a person's soul. This conflict leads the person toward religion or spiritual meditation. Using these two mediums, the person tries to live by the best morals he knows. No matter how good a person tries to live, as long as the spirit is dead, God considers that goodness as filthy rags because it originates from the soul and not from the spirit.

A MANDATE FROM GOD

For they that are after the flesh do mind the things of the flesh; but they that are after the Spirit the things of the Spirit. For to be carnally minded is death; but to be spiritually minded is life and peace. Because the carnal mind is enmity against God: for it is not subject to the law of God, neither indeed can be. So then they that are in the flesh cannot please God.

— Rom. 8:5-8

God expects that every person should live by his spirit and not by his soul. Living by the soul is also referred to as living in the flesh or walking in the flesh. When you live by the spirit, the soul is influenced by godly matters. When you live by the soul, the same is either influenced by the body or relies on the conscience or emotions to make the right decision. Since the spirit in a person is dead, how can this be achieved? This can only be achieved when the person experiences a new birth in the spirit. The new birth does not mean we should be physically born from our mother's womb again, but it means to be spiritually born by placing our faith in Jesus Christ.

CHAPTER 3

The Second Birth

KINGDOM OF GOD

And when he was demanded of the Pharisees, when the kingdom of God should come, he answered them and said, The kingdom of God cometh not with observation: neither shall they say, Lo here! or, lo there! for, behold, the kingdom of God is within you.

– Luk. 17:20, 21

The term "kingdom of God" or "kingdom of heaven" implies God's rule in a specific domain. We all know that God rules in heaven, and so His kingdom is in heaven. However, Jesus promised to His disciples that He would send His Holy Spirit within them, and they would experience the kingdom of God within them. It implies that anyone who has received Jesus Christ as their Lord and Savior would receive the Holy Spirit within them, and they would experience the kingdom of God within their life. As the Holy Spirit begins to take control of a person, the character of the person will begin to take shape according to the character of Christ. When the nature of Christ is imprinted on a person, they need not make any effort to keep the laws of God, for they are already keeping them as part of their new nature. When a person gives complete control of their life to the Holy Spirit, they are acknowledging that Jesus Christ is truly the Lord of their life. Unless you let Jesus be the Lord of your life, you cannot truly experience the kingdom of God within you.

ATONEMENT FOR OUR SINS

Much more then, being now justified by his blood, we shall be saved from wrath through him.

– Rom. 5:9

The Bible says that the entire human race has fallen short of God's moral standards. This is because every person in this world has inherited the sin and curse of Adam by birth. Due to this, every person is inherently a sinner, and we have been disconnected from God. Even our own sins have made us enemies of God. Not only did God curse Adam, but He also declared a curse on every sinner. Moreover, Satan took advantage of our sins and curses, and he kept us in bondage to various wrong habits and addictions. The only way out of this dilemma was for God to send His only begotten Son, Jesus Christ, into this earth to die for our sins on the cross of Calvary. The shed blood of Jesus paved the way for us to get reconnected to God once again because the Father was pleased with the sinless sacrifice of Jesus. The blood of Jesus was the perfect atonement for our sins.

JESUS: THE LAST ADAM, AND THE SECOND MAN

And so it is written, The first man Adam was made a living soul; the last Adam was made a quickening spirit.

The first man is of the earth, earthy: the second man is the Lord from heaven.

– 1 Cor. 15:45,47

When Jesus came into this world, he represented mankind in two ways. As the Last Adam, he came to eliminate the sin and curse of Adam that had passed on to all generations after Adam. He did eliminate them when he died on the cross and shed his precious blood for the remission of sins of mankind. As believers, we appropriated it in the form of water baptism. As we were water baptised, we were freed from the sin and curse of Adam, and our Adamic nature was put to death. As a Second Man, Jesus began a new race in this world when he rose up from the dead. According to this new race, people can now be born of God by accepting Jesus Christ as their Lord and Savior, and follow him to guide our life. Therefore, anyone who has put their faith in Jesus Christ is dead to the sin and curse of Adam by Jesus being the Last Adam, and the person is born again to live according to God's precepts by Jesus being the Second Man.

BE BORN AGAIN

Jesus answered and said unto him, Verily, verily, I say unto thee, Except a man be born again, he cannot see the kingdom of God.

That which is born of the flesh is flesh; and that which is born of the Spirit is spirit.

– John 3:3,6

Jesus, in his discourse with Nicodemus says that in order to see the kingdom of God, a person must be born again. Then he further explains that to be born again is to be born of the spirit. Our natural birth is that of the flesh when we were born of our parents. Our second birth must be through the Spirit of God. When we were born of our parents, we were born with natural instincts such as having love for food, clothing, education, family, friends, job, sports, etc. but when we are born of the spirit, we will have spiritual instincts for prayer, worship, Bible reading, and so on.

Many people display the spiritual instincts without being born again, but that is not the right approach to reach out to God. In John 4:23-24, Jesus tells the Samaritan woman, *"But the hour cometh, and now is, when the true worshippers shall worship the Father in spirit and in truth: for the Father seeketh such to worship him. God is a Spirit: and they that worship him must worship him in spirit and in truth."* Since God is a spirit being, those who worship him must also worship in the spirit and not in the natural. No person will be able to worship God in the spirit unless the person is born again. Jesus also says that the person must worship in truth. Truth is biblical knowledge revealed by the Holy Spirit. Unless the person is born again, he or she will not know the truth. In other words, the Holy Spirit will reveal the truth of his Word only to those who are born again.

When a person connects to God by means of worship in spirit and in truth, God will impart his spiritual treasure within the person which enables the person to experience the kingdom of God within him or her.

STEPS TO BE BORN AGAIN

1. REPENTANCE

> *Repent ye therefore, and be converted, that your sins may be blotted out, when the times of refreshing shall come from the presence of the Lord.*
>
> *– Acts 3:19*

Even though Jesus did offer His blood as the perfect atonement for our sins, we cannot receive forgiveness from God unless we repent of our sins. Repentance is the gateway to forgiveness. True repentance is to forsake our current lifestyle and adopt the ways of God. It is to make a commitment to change our lives as instructed by God. Repentance brings reconciliation with God.

2. ACKNOWLEDGING JESUS AS LORD

> *That if thou shalt confess with thy mouth the Lord Jesus, and shalt believe in thine heart that God hath raised him from the dead, thou shalt be saved. For with the heart man believeth unto righteousness; and with the mouth confession is made unto salvation.*
>
> *– Rom. 10:9, 10*

When you confess that Jesus Christ is Lord and believe in your heart that God raised Him from the dead, you will be saved. When you confess, you enter into a covenant with God in which you are required to live by faith, and God has promised to assist you in maintaining the expected holiness. Until you make that confession, your spirit remains dead because of sins, and your body alone influences your soul. But the moment you make that confession, your spirit is made alive and enables it to communicate with the Holy Spirit. Also, the Holy Spirit begins to live in you to guide you and teach you the things of God. Your spirit will now be able to influence your soul on godly matters. In other words, you can say that you are now born in the spirit. This is your rebirth.

3. BE WASHED BY THE BLOOD OF JESUS

In whom we have redemption through his blood, the forgiveness of sins, according to the riches of his grace.

– Eph. 1:7

After we have repented of our sins, and accepted Jesus Christ as our Lord and Savior, we must ask God to forgive us our sins by means of the precious blood that Jesus shed on the cross. Since Jesus atoned for our soul by means of his own blood, our heavenly Father will forgive us from all our sins. Since the life of a person is in the blood, the blood is the ultimate price one can pay for our life, and Jesus did just that. Thus, our soul is saved.

4. WATER BAPTISM

Know ye not, that so many of us as were baptized into Jesus Christ were baptized into his death?

knowing this, that our old man is crucified with him, that the body of sin might be destroyed, that henceforth we should not serve sin. For he that is dead is freed from sin.

– Rom. 6:3, 6, 7

Even though you are now born again, your body is still able to influence your soul because we have not taken care of the body. As your body came from the Adamic lineage, you still have the nature of sin and the associated curse in your body. The only way for your body not to influence your soul is to put your body to death. This is symbolically done by what is known as water baptism. Water baptism is a means by which you identify yourself as being dead when Jesus died on the cross. The death of your body implies death to the Adamic nature in you. Your death is symbolized by your immersion in water. As you immerse in water, it implies that you are being buried along with Christ. As you come out of the water, you will no longer have the Adamic nature in you. You become a new creature in Christ Jesus.

APPLYING THE STEPS

Now that you know the steps to be born again, how do you actually apply it in your own life? It begins by prayer of repentance. This prayer covers the first three steps mentioned above which is repentance, accepting Jesus as Lord, and getting washed by the blood of Jesus. This prayer can be made anywhere, but it is better to make it in the presence of witnesses such as in a church setting or in a house fellowship. The prayer goes something like this: *"Heavenly Father, I come before your throne of grace and I repent of every sin that I have committed against you knowingly or unknowingly in my thoughts, words, and deeds and I ask you to forgive me from all my sins. I believe that you sent your only begotten son Jesus Christ into this world, who died for my sins on the cross of calvary, and I can be forgiven by the blood he shed on the cross. So Father, I ask you to wash me clean with the precious blood of Jesus and make me clean from every sin. I acknowledge Jesus Christ as my personal Lord and Savior and I believe in my heart that God raised him from the dead. Now that you have forgiven me, I ask you to send your Holy Spirit to live within me and I believe that I am born again. From this day forward, I surrender my life to you and serve you all the days of my life, as I am led by the Holy Spirit. In Jesus' name I pray. Amen."* As for water baptism, you need to ask your church pastor or an elder to help you get water baptized.

A NEW CREATURE

Therefore if any man be in Christ, he is a new creature: old things are passed away; behold, all things are become new.

– 2 Cor. 5:17

Having been born again, the Bible calls you a new creature. The Adamic sins and curses in you have been erased from your life, and you have been born of the Holy Spirit. You are now a child of God. You can now communicate with God by means of the Holy Spirit. God is no longer mad at you. You are at peace with God. From this point forward, the Holy Spirit will lead you and guide you to walk in the ways of God.

A NEW IDENTITY

When we accepted Jesus Christ as our Lord and Savior, the Holy Spirit came to live within us, and we became new people. Having become born again, we have also inherited a new identity. As per this new identity, we are adopted by God to be His own children. Because we are His children, we are loved by Him, and He is always with us. He has saved us, and we are no longer condemned. He has healed us from our sickness and set us free from our curses. He has broken every bondage to sin, and He has made us victorious over the powers of darkness.

CHAPTER 4

Wholesome Salvation

THE CONCEPT OF SALVATION

The Bible declares in Rom. 3:23 saying, *"For all have sinned, and come short of the glory of God"*. In Rom. 6:23, the Bible says, *"For the wages of sin is death; but the gift of God is eternal life through Jesus Christ our Lord."* These two scriptures tell us that there is no person on earth who is just and righteous, which means every one of us were destined for hell. But God in his mercy sent Jesus Christ to die for our sins on the cross of calvary so that whoever believes in him may not perish but shall have everlasting life. This free gift of God that gives us everlasting life is called "Salvation". This gift is not reserved for the privileged few, but to anyone who recognizes the need and takes the necessary steps mentioned earlier. By means of salvation, God adopts us as His own children, and lives inside of us to teach and guide us, so that we may continuously live according to God's will. Salvation involves:

1. Forgiveness of our sins
2. Replacing our curses with blessings
3. Freedom from sickness, disease, infirmity, and death
4. Freedom from oppression and torment by demons

THE THREE TENSES

The Bible speaks of salvation in three tenses as follows:

- "We are saved" is the present tense.
- "We are being saved" is the present continuous tense.
- "We will be saved" is a future tense.

Because of these three tenses, many Christians are confused, not knowing if they are already saved, or if they are being saved, or if they will be saved sometime in the future. Bible teachers explain these tenses as follows:

"We are saved": This is justification. To be justified means to stand right in the sight of God. This righteousness is offered to us freely by God by means of the precious blood of Jesus as we accept the lordship of Jesus over our lives and believe in the death and resurrection of Jesus Christ.

"We are being saved": This is sanctification. Sanctification is the process by which our sinful nature is progressively removed from us, thereby we are being transformed into the image of Christ. This progressive change happens in our lives as we keep walking by faith and not by our five natural senses.

"We will be saved": This is glorification. Glorification is an event whereby we will be taken to heaven, either by means of death or by the rapture. The Bible says that all those who are born again will be taken to heaven when our life on this earth is over.

THE SALVATION PROCESS

In order to solve the confusion around the tenses mentioned above, let us see how the salvation process works. The first four steps of the salvation process are the four steps of rebirth mentioned in the previous chapter. Besides that, there are three more steps that we need to take on a frequent basis. Certain steps will have to be revisited as we live our daily life here on earth.

Being born again is one-time experience where our spirit, soul, and body are all saved. However, we do fall into sin because of our own weaknesses. One of the weaknesses is our lack of the knowledge of God's will. We must know what God thinks about any aspect of our life. We must know what pleases God and what displeases him.

The second weakness we find in ourselves is the urge to commit sin. Because of this urge, we are not able to come in agreement with God's will concerning certain evil. We consider certain evil not to be evil because we find pleasure out of it. Since God has already passed his judgment or verdict concerning evil, we cannot act otherwise. We must align with the will of God. Even if our mind thinks not to commit sin, our body pushes us to commit certain sins. Only after we have committed the sin, we feel satisfied. This is where we need to know how to crucify the flesh.

If we ever fall into sin by reason of not knowing the will of God, or by not coming into agreement with the will of God, or by the urge within us to commit sin, both our soul and body gets defiled, and we must work our way out to bring our soul and body back to holiness, and this is done by repenting of our sins, and partaking in the communion.

The KNOWLEDGE OF GOD's WILL

And be not conformed to this world: but be ye transformed by the renewing of your mind, that ye may prove what is that good, and acceptable, and perfect, will of God.

– Rom. 12:2

As of now, we have seen two processes taking place in you. First, your spirit was made alive, which influences your soul in godly matters. Second, your body was put to death, which causes your body not to influence our soul anymore. It appears that your soul is now free from any bad influence because your body has been put to death and your spirit has been made alive. But this fact still does not guarantee that your soul is free from any bad influence. You still have your mind, which has registered all the good and bad deeds that can still influence your soul. Just because a certain idea is bad, that does not necessarily mean your soul will reject it. Every thought you receive will stir up your emotions, and if that emotion is a pleasure, you will entertain that thought. If the emotion is pain, you will reject that thought. Your past experiences determine if something is a pain or a pleasure to you. All of our pleasures need not necessarily be God's will. Similarly, all of our pains need not necessarily be God's displeasure. For this reason, you should now exercise the ability to switch certain pleasures into pain and certain pains into pleasure so that they may align with God's pleasures and displeasures. This switching is done when you spend your time reading the Bible. It is called meditating on the Word of God. Anything that displeases God should be your pain, and anything that pleases God should be your pleasure. It is an exercise that transforms you into the image of Christ and will not let you conform to the lifestyle of this world.

CRUCIFYING THE FLESH

If any man come to me, and hate not his father, and mother, and wife, and children, and brethren, and sisters, yea, and his own life also, he cannot be my disciple. And whosoever doth not bear his cross, and come after me, cannot be my disciple.

– Luke 14:26-27

The reason why we cannot come into agreement with God's will is because we are being influenced by our blood relatives and friends, and even our own selfish desires. Unless we defeat these influencing factors from influencing us to do things that are contrary to God's will, we will not be able to stay righteous. Mark 8:38 says, *"Whosoever therefore shall be ashamed of me and of my words in this adulterous and sinful generation; of him also shall the Son of man be ashamed, when he cometh in the glory of his Father with the holy angels."* The reason why we allow our near and dear ones to influence us is because we are ashamed to stand alongside Jesus come what may.

COMMUNION

The cup of blessing which we bless, is it not the communion of the blood of Christ? The bread which we break, is it not the communion of the body of Christ?

– 1 Cor. 10:16

Whenever the soul gives in to the demands of the body, it becomes defiled, and the person's salvation is at stake. In such moments, we must repent of our sins and participate in what is known as communion. Communion is the practice of eating bread and drinking wine after they have been sanctified by the elders of the church. Once sanctified, the bread represents the broken body of Jesus Christ, and the wine represents the blood of Jesus Christ. While the broken body of Jesus brings healing to our ailing bodies, the blood brings forgiveness for the sins we have committed. We must understand that whenever we fall into sin, both our soul and our body become defiled, and the practice of communion will restore us back to our salvation.

STEPS TO SALVATION

Let us recap on the steps to salvation:

Step 1: Repentance from sins

Step 2: Acknowledge Jesus Christ as Lord and Savior

Step 3: Be washed by the blood

Step 4: Water baptism

Step 5: Knowledge of God's will

Step 6: Crucifying the Flesh

Step 7: Communion

Step 1 (*Repentance from sins*) is the precondition to salvation. People can fail in step 1 when they don't realize that they are sinners or if they do not want to acknowledge that they are sinners. People also fail in step 1 if they do not want to change their lifestyle, customs, culture, religion, etc.

Step 2 (*Acknowledge Jesus Christ as Lord and Savior*) saves the person in their spirit, and this salvation is permanent as long as the person places his or her faith in the Lord Jesus Christ.

Step 3 (*Be Washed by the Blood*) saves the person in their soul as they place their faith in the shed blood of Jesus. At this point, since the body has not been saved and is still under the control of Adamic sinful nature, the body will influence the soul to pursue material things. As the soul indulges in material things, both the soul and the body get defiled, but not the spirit. The spirit remains saved as long as the person continues to believe in Jesus Christ.

Step 4 (*Water baptism*) puts our Adamic body to death. It is not a literal death but a symbolic one. The purpose of this step is to prevent the body from influencing the soul to pursue material things. Since steps 2 and 3 have saved the spirit and the soul, step 4 completes the process of getting the body saved as well. At this point, your spirit, soul, and body are all saved.

Step 5 (*Knowledge of God's will*) is required to be kept because we continue to fall into sin despite the fact that our spirit, soul, and body are all saved. When we know the will of God, we will be cautious not to violate the will of God. Unless we have this knowledge, we will not be aware if we are committing any sin against God.

Step 6 (*Crucifying the Flesh*) is about denying our pleasures and our will to be operated in our lives and allowing God to rule our lives as per his will. The reason why we fall into sin is because of our past experiences, which are registered in our soul. We have various experiences of pleasure and pain prior to our salvation. Unless the pattern of pleasure and pain is aligned with that of God, we will continue to fall into sin. Besides that, we are also being influenced by our blood relatives to do things contrary to the will of God. If we have to please God at all times, then it is incumbent on us to deny all of the influencing factors that includes our own will as well.

Step 7 (*Communion*) is mandated by Jesus to be observed by every Christian as it restores us back in alignment with God whenever we fall out of alignment. Communion sanctifies our body and soul once again so we can have a right standing with God. Once we are done with step 7, we must go back to step 5 to continue living by God's will and not by our will.

THREE-FOLD SALVATION

And the very God of peace sanctify you wholly; and I pray God your whole spirit and soul and body be preserved blameless unto the coming of our Lord Jesus Christ.

– 1 Thes. 5:23

The Bible demands that we must be saved in our spirit, soul, and body and should not be caught unaware when Jesus comes back again to lift His church unto Himself. Therefore, it is essential that we know how to be saved in each of these areas.

SALVATION OF OUR SPIRIT

But God, who is rich in mercy, for his great love wherewith he loved us, Even when we were dead in sins, hath quickened us together with Christ, (by grace ye are saved;)

– Eph. 2:4-5

We are saved in the spirit when we confess Jesus Christ as Lord, and believe in our hearts that God raised Him from the dead. To be saved in the spirit implies that our spirit, which was dead earlier because of sins, has now been made alive. This is the salvation of our spirit. The salvation of our spirit is permanent and will never be undone unless we deny Jesus Christ as our Lord and Savior. When we are saved in the spirit, the Holy Spirit comes and resides in our hearts. The Holy Spirit will then begin to guide us and teach us the things of God.

To understand why the salvation of our spirit is permanent, we need to look at Rom. 5:19 which says, *"For as by one man's disobedience many were made sinners, so by the obedience of one shall many be made righteous."* Here, the Bible says that the effect of Adam's sin caused the rest of mankind to become sinners, regardless of whether they committed sin or not. The same law would now apply when it comes to Jesus' obedience. The righteousness of Jesus would cause everyone who believe in him to inherit his righteousness whether or not they lived a righteous life. Since this righteousness came to us as a free gift, it will never be taken away. The only way for the salvation of the spirit to be terminated is apostasy.

SALVATION OF OUR SOUL

> *Whom God hath set forth to be a propitiation through faith in his blood, to declare his righteousness for the remission of sins that are past, through the forbearance of God.*
>
> *– Rom. 3:25*

As per the scripture above, we are saved in our soul when we place our faith in the shed blood of Jesus Christ for the forgiveness of our sins. However, the salvation of our soul is conditional in the sense that if we ever fall into sin, the salvation of our soul will be at stake. We will have to repent of our sins and partake of the communion to get in alignment with God's righteousness once again. The salvation of our soul is maintained by our walk of faith. As long as we walk by faith, the salvation of our souls is intact. The moment we fall into sin, it implies that we failed to walk by faith.

Lev. 17:11 says, *"For the life of the flesh is in the blood: and I have given it to you upon the altar to make an atonement for your souls: for it is the blood that maketh an atonement for the soul."* Since the blood atones for our soul, our faith in the blood of Jesus brings salvation to our soul. The blood of the animals in the Old Testament only covered the sins of the people because of which it had to be offered over and over again, and yet it did not eliminate their sin. However, according to Heb. 10:14, *"For by one offering he hath perfected for ever them that are sanctified."* The sacrifice of Jesus was so perfect that it required to be offered only once for the forgiveness of sins of mankind.

SALVATION OF OUR BODY

Buried with him in baptism, wherein also ye are risen with him through the faith of the operation of God, who hath raised him from the dead.

– Col. 2:12

We will be saved in our bodies when we are water-baptized. Water baptism signifies our death to the Adamic nature in us, and we will rise up as new creatures. From then on, we need to reckon that we are dead indeed to sin and alive in righteousness. The fact that we are dead to our Adamic nature remains permanent. We fall into sin when we fail to reckon the fact that our body is dead to sin, and we live in righteousness. We should then repent of our sins and partake of the communion to get right with God.

According to Rom. 6:6-7, the Bible says, *"Knowing this, that our old man is crucified with him, that the body of sin might be destroyed, that henceforth we should not serve sin. For he that is dead is freed from sin."* So, baptism signifies dying alongside Jesus and also rising up along with Jesus.

THE THIEF ON THE CROSS

And he said unto Jesus, Lord, remember me when thou comest into thy kingdom. And Jesus said unto him, Verily I say unto thee, To day shalt thou be with me in paradise.

– Luk. 23:42, 43

Many Christians consider water baptism to be just symbolic, and it adds no value to our salvation. That is because they say that the thief who was hung on the cross besides Jesus was not baptized, yet Jesus promised to take him to paradise. We must understand that the thief was in his dying moments. He did not have to live his life on earth anymore. Therefore, there is no way he could fall into sin again. For this reason, it was not required for him to be baptized. However, in our case, once we are saved in our spirit and in our soul by means of confessing Jesus Christ as Lord and believing in our hearts that God raised him from the dead, we continue to live our lives here on earth. At this point, since our body is not saved due to not having taken water baptism, the Adamic nature in us will force us to commit sin. But if we had taken the water baptism, the Adamic nature in us would have been eliminated, and there would have been no one forcing us to commit sin. When we are water baptized, we are dead to Adamic nature and to sin, making us free to choose and follow righteousness. Another way to look at it is that baptism signifies our death along with Jesus. Since the thief on the cross did die along with Jesus, that very fact signifies that he was baptized in the death of Jesus.

CHAPTER 5

Living By Faith

THE CONDITIONAL SALVATION

But that no man is justified by the law in the sight of God, it is evident: for, The just shall live by faith.

— Gal. 3:11

From the earlier chapters, we understand that the salvation of our spirit is permanent, while the salvation of our soul and body is conditional. To maintain the salvation of our souls, we must walk by faith. Walking by faith implies believing in who Jesus is, His sacrifice on the cross, the redemption of our sins by His blood, our new identity in Christ, and our victorious future. If we ever fail to walk by faith, we will be defiled in our souls and body. The condition to keep the salvation of both the soul and the body in such a state is to repent of our sins, and partake of the communion.

WALKING IN THE SPIRIT

There is therefore now no condemnation to them which are in Christ Jesus, who walk not after the flesh, but after the Spirit.

— Rom. 8:1

Every person who is born again has two lives. He can either live by his soul or by his spirit. The Bible commands that we always walk in the spirit. John 4:23 says, *"But the hour cometh, and now is, when the true worshippers shall worship the Father in spirit and in truth: for the Father seeketh such to worship him."* It is worship that connects us to God in the spirit. Our worship should not be done in the natural, but in the spirit. Also, our worship should not be done being ignorant of the Word of God. We must have the basic revelation of the Word of God as we worship. When we spend our time in the presence of the Lord through prayer, worship, and meditating on the Word of God, we will be transformed from the soulish world to the spiritual world. Sometimes, we may not be able to connect to God because of the hardness of our heart. In such situations, we may even have to fast while we connect to God. It is also beneficial to use the gift of speaking in tongues as we pray to God. Our faith can only be exercised when we are in the spiritual world. Being in the soulish world, we will not be able to exercise our faith. Therefore, it is essential that we walk in the spirit to live by faith. The scripture above says that when we walk in the spirit, we are "in Christ", and only when we are "in Christ", we are not condemned.

CHRIST IN US, AND WE IN CHRIST

I am the vine, ye are the branches: He that abideth in me, and I in him, the same bringeth forth much fruit: for without me ye can do nothing.

– John 15:5

When we are born again, the Holy Spirit comes and stays in our heart. This fact is called "Christ in us". The Holy Spirit is always there to guide us and to teach us to walk in the ways of God. At the same time, God expects that we too walk with Christ. This event is called "We in Christ". All the promises of God are fulfilled in our life only when we are "in Christ". As we saw earlier that when we walk in the spirit, we are always "in Christ". Therefore, it is essential that if we want to live the abundant life of Christ, we must always walk in the spirit. Rom.

8:13 says, *"For if ye live after the flesh, ye shall die: but if ye through the Spirit do mortify the deeds of the body, ye shall live."* The goal of walking in the spirit is to mortify the deeds of our body. That is, to put our flesh to death which can also be called as "crucifying our flesh". The flesh is our bad behaviour. Gal. 5:16 says, *"This I say then, Walk in the Spirit, and ye shall not fulfil the lust of the flesh."* So, this scripture assures us that when we walk in the spirit, we will not fulfil the desires of the flesh.

THE SOUL AND THE FLESH

People who are not born again cannot live in the spirit, for their spirit is dead because of sin. They can only live in the soul. In other words, they can only live a natural life and not a supernatural life. As their spirit is dead, their soul can only be influenced by their body, which contacts the material world. There is no way their soul can receive anything from God. They can only receive things from the material world through their body or good morals through their conscience. Therefore, their entire soul is made of flesh.

A born-again person, on the other hand, is able to walk in the spirit since his spirit is made alive. As the person walks in the spirit, he is able to exercise faith and live a holy life. That does not mean that a born-again person cannot fall into sin. He definitely falls into sin because he still has what is known as flesh. Flesh is that part of the soul that is not in alignment with God's will. Walking in the flesh could also mean living in the natural realm or the soulish realm. To live in the soul is to live a natural life. Living in the spirit is to live a supernatural life. God demands that we always walk in the spirit and not in the flesh. When we walk in the flesh, we succumb to temptations and sin. When we walk in the spirit, we will never give in to temptation, nor will we fall into sin. If any person falls into sin, it is only because he is not walking in the spirit. Walking in the flesh does not necessarily mean living in sin. It can also mean living according to good morals based on one's conscience. Any goodness that originates from the soul is still unrighteous in the sight of God. The goodness that originates from the spirit alone can be considered righteous. Our emotions play a greater role in catering to the flesh. If our emotions find a thought enjoyable, our soul will respond to it. If our emotions find a thought to be painful, our soul will reject it. What we consider pleasure and pain need not necessarily be God's pleasure or pain.

REASONS TO OVERCOME FLESH

If a man abide not in me, he is cast forth as a branch, and is withered; and men gather them, and cast them into the fire, and they are burned.

– John 15:6

Flesh stands as a hindrance to doing God's will in our lives. Unless the flesh is defeated, we will not be able to serve God. If we allow sin to rule our lives, God himself will place enemies in our lives to torment us. But torment should not be a reason to overcome flesh. The reason why we should overcome the flesh and live a godly life is to help millions of people who are suffering in their own ways and are looking for a Savior. As God's children, we can be a channel of help for all such people. As we keep crucifying our flesh, we develop the character of Christ in us. The Bible calls it the fruit of the Holy Spirit, which is comprised of love, joy, peace, patience, gentleness, goodness, faith, meekness, and self-control. When this new nature becomes part of our lives, it is as if we have kept the laws of God. Therefore, keeping the laws of God should be a part of our new nature rather than trying to keep them while our flesh is still alive in us. The more we crucify our flesh, the more Christ will be able to live his life through us. In other words, Jesus will have a free hand in our lives to make us live according to his will. The life of Christ manifested through our lives is what brings true salvation to our lives.

SALVATION BY FAITH

*For by grace are ye saved through faith; and that not of yourselves:
it is the gift of God: not of works, lest any man should boast.*

– Eph. 2:8, 9

In the scripture above, the word "saved" means salvation. The word "grace" means God's power that works on behalf of us. The word "faith" means to believe and to receive Jesus Christ as our Lord and Savior. So, the meaning of the entire verse is that God, by the power of his grace, enabled us to place our faith in Jesus Christ, through whom we received salvation. This salvation was given as a gift to us. We could not have earned it through our efforts. If we could, we would have had a reason to boast.

Faith is to believe in the facts that brought about our salvation. These are the facts that we believe in:

1. Jesus is the Son of God. The term "Son of God" implies that He is God incarnated in human form.
2. Jesus offered Himself as a sacrifice for our sins on the cross of Calvary.
3. By the shed blood of Jesus, our sins are forgiven.
4. Jesus was resurrected from the dead on the third day.

What was the outcome of our faith as we believed in Jesus Christ, and what happened as we took water baptism?

1. Our spirit, which was dead, was made alive, and it is now able to influence our soul on godly matters.
2. Our body, which was influencing our soul on matters pertaining to material things, was put to death as we took water baptism. Therefore, the body can no longer influence our soul anymore as it is dead.
3. The Holy Spirit has come within us and is now guiding us to walk in God's will.

Besides the facts listed above, we also should know that our soul can make its own decision to violate the will of God based on the concept of pleasure and pain. Because of this, our actions may be contrary to the will of God. We must exercise our minds to believe that God's Word is true regardless of how we feel about it. We must overcome our emotions by means of fasting and prayer and abide by the will of God as stated in the Bible. Our negative thoughts and our dire circumstances can make us to give up our faith. To walk this challenging walk of faith, we must know and affirm our new identity in Christ.

THE ARMOR OF GOD

> *Be sober, be vigilant; because your adversary the devil, as a roaring lion, walketh about, seeking whom he may devour: whom resist stedfast in the faith, knowing that the same afflictions are accomplished in your brethren that are in the world.*

> *– 1 Pet. 5:8, 9*

As we believe in our new identity in Christ, Satan challenges this belief by placing doubts in our minds. This is when we should wear the armor and pick up our weapons of warfare to wage war against these doubts. If we are not vigilant enough, then Satan can bring destruction into our lives. Therefore, we must wear the following six pieces of armor and be vigilant against any sort of bad influence over us:

1. Belt of Truth

   To have the revelation knowledge of the Word of God.

2. Breastplate of Righteousness

   To know that you have already been made righteous.

3. Shoes worn and prepared to preach the gospel of peace.

   To be ready like a soldier and committed to preach.

4. Shield of Faith

   To confront challenging circumstances with the Word of God.

5. Helmet of Salvation

    To know that you have already been saved.

6. Sword of the Spirit, which is the Word of God

    To bind and to loose, in the name of Jesus, using the Word of God.

Using the armor mentioned above, we need to fight the good fight of faith. In other words, we must affirm that we continue to believe in the Word of God despite our circumstances. For example, Adam was already created in the image of God, but Satan tricked Eve by saying, "you will be like gods." Similarly, Satan can trick us into believing by saying, "if you do such and such things, you will be saved," while we are already saved.

OUR AUTHORITY AS A BELIEVER

And these signs shall follow them that believe; In my name shall they cast out devils; they shall speak with new tongues; they shall take up serpents; and if they drink any deadly thing, it shall not hurt them; they shall lay hands on the sick, and they shall recover.

– Mark 16:17, 18

As we got born again, Jesus restored the authority in us that Adam and Eve had lost. Using the spiritual weapons described here, we can defeat Satan and subdue his power. Even though Jesus disarmed Satan on the cross, we, as the followers of Christ, must enforce that victory by walking in faith and fighting the good fight of faith.

THE WEAPONS OF WARFARE

For we wrestle not against flesh and blood, but against principalities, against powers, against the rulers of the darkness of this world, against spiritual wickedness in high places.

– Eph. 6:12

Our battle is not against humans but against the wicked spirits in the heavenly realm. Therefore, we do not use physical weapons to fight but spiritual ones. The spiritual weapons that we use are the blood, the Word or the Truth, the Name of Jesus, and our Testimonies.

1. THE BLOOD

In whom we have redemption through his blood, the forgiveness of sins, according to the riches of his grace;

– Eph. 1:7

When Jesus died on the cross, he defeated the devil by means of the blood that he shed. He made a divine exchange on the cross by reversing everything that was against us:

- Jesus was punished, that we might be forgiven.
- Jesus was wounded, that we might be healed.

  - (Isaiah 53:4-5)

- Jesus was made sin with our sinfulness, that we might be made righteous with His righteousness.

  - (Isaiah 53:10, 2 Corinthians 5:21)

- Jesus died our death, that we might receive His life.

  - (Heb. 2:9)

- Jesus was made a curse, that we might enter into the blessing.

  - (Galatians 3:13-14)

- Jesus endured our poverty, that we might share His abundance.
  – (2 Corinthians 8:9, 2 Corinthians 9:8)
- Jesus bore our shame, that we might share His glory.

  - (Matthew 27:35-36, Hebrews 12:2, Hebrews 2:9)

- Jesus endured rejection, that we might have His acceptance with the Father.

    - (Matthew 27:46-51, Ephesians 1:5-6, Isaiah 53:8)

- Jesus was cut off by death that we might be joined to God eternally.

    - (Isaiah 53:8, 1 Corinthians 6:17)

- Our old man was put to death in Him that the new man might come to life in us.

    - (Romans 6:6, Colossians 3:9-10)

We must believe that we are forgiven of our sins, we are healed from our sicknesses, we are made righteous with the righteousness of Jesus Christ, our spirit has been resurrected, we are blessed, we are made rich in every aspect, we are honored, we are accepted by God the Father, we are joined with the Lord, we are made anew. Now, this is an established fact, and nothing in this world can negate it.

2. THE TRUTH

Then said Jesus to those Jews which believed on him, If ye continue in my word, then are ye my disciples indeed; and ye shall know the truth, and the truth shall make you free.

– John 8:31, 32

When the Word of God is revealed to us, it becomes the truth. When we know the truth, it will set us free, primarily from ignorance. When Satan came to tempt Jesus in the wilderness, Jesus confronted him with the Word of God. This is how we can keep ourselves from stumbling. As we spend much time meditating on the Word of God, God will give us the revelation knowledge of the Word we are reading. As we keep applying his Word in our own lives consistently, we will know more of his Truth.

3. THE NAME OF JESUS

Wherefore God also hath highly exalted him, and given him a name which is above every name: that at the name of Jesus every knee should bow, of things in heaven, and things in earth, and things under the earth; and that every tongue should confess that Jesus Christ is Lord, to the glory of God the Father.

– Phi. 2:9-11

When Jesus rose from the dead, he received all authority and power in heaven and on earth from his heavenly Father. Since the Holy Spirit is living within us, it is as good as saying Jesus is living within us. We must understand that Jesus who conquered death and grave is now living within us. When we use the name of Jesus, the authority and power that Jesus received is put into action and every circumstance that is challenging us will cease to exist.

4. OUR TESTIMONIES

And they overcame him by the blood of the Lamb, and by the word of their testimony; and they loved not their lives unto the death.

– Rev. 12:11

As we keep declaring our testimony as to how God delivered us and saved us, it crumbles every stronghold of the enemy. The scripture above tells us that our testimonies are so powerful that it can even unseat Satan from his throne. As we declare our testimonies, angels will fight on our behalf and give us the victory.

GOSPEL IN A NUTSHELL

Let us inspect our lives pre-salvation, post-salvation, and at the time of salvation. *Prior to our salvation,* our spirit was dead because of Adam's sins. We had no relationship with God. We all committed sins and we were the enemies of God. *At the time of salvation,* the Adamic sins and curses were broken from off our lives, and we were completely saved in our spirit, soul, and body. However, our past memories, emotions, and conscience still remain the same which can be called as flesh. *Post-salvation*, we are called to defeat our flesh, and maintain the salvation we have freely received from God by means of worship, prayer, fasting, and meditation of the Word of God. As we meditate on the Word of God, our mind is reprogrammed and retrained to live in holiness as demanded by God. Our worship, prayer, and fasting enables us to connect to God and walk in the spirit. As we walk in the spirit, we will be able to walk by faith, and are able to confront the enemy that takes advantage of our weaknesses in the flesh.

Prior to our salvation, Jesus took the place of our penalty of death on the cross. Post-salvation, Jesus takes the place of our life to obey God in all aspects. However, whether Jesus would live his life in and through us or not depends on the free-will we exercise on a daily basis.

CHAPTER 6

Sin and Reconciliation

THE SUBTILITY OF SIN

Sin enters our life in many different forms. Jam. 4:17 says, *"Therefore to him that knoweth to do good, and doeth it not, to him it is sin."* Sometimes, our pride takes over and we neglect to listen to the voice of the Holy Spirit within us. There are sins of commission and sins of omission. The sins of commission are wrongful acts that a person actively commits, such as lying, stealing, or idolatry. It involves an action that directly violates God's commandments. The sins of omission occur when a person fails to do something good or right that they ought to do. An example might include failing to help someone in need or neglecting to pray or worship God. No matter what kind of sins we may have committed, we must ask forgiveness from God if we are to be reconciled with him.

THE EFFECTS OF SIN

And said, If thou wilt diligently hearken to the voice of the LORD thy God, and wilt do that which is right in his sight, and wilt give ear to his commandments, and keep all his statutes, I will put none of these diseases upon thee, which I have brought upon the Egyptians: for I am the LORD that healeth thee.

– Exo. 15:26

Sin always results in sickness and bondage. Healing from sickness, and deliverance from bondage, is part of the salvation of the body. As we repent of our sins and partake of the communion, we will not only be forgiven of our sins, but we will be healed from our sicknesses. As for the deliverance from bondage, it takes the anointing of the Holy Spirit to cast the evil spirits out of our body. Wherever the Bible refers to healing and deliverance, the Greek word used in this case is "sozo" which means "salvation" or "saved".

CONFESSION OF SINS

As we walk by faith, there are times when we forget to walk in the spirit and instead, we walk in the flesh. When challenging circumstances come toward us, we will not have the ability to fight by faith. This is when we give in to those challenges, and this is when we commit sin. Sin defiles our soul and our body but not our spirit. Our spirit continues to remain saved because we still believe in Jesus. Because our spirit is still saved, we still hold our identity and our position in Christ. However, our souls and bodies have been defiled, and we need to reconcile with God.

> *If we confess our sins, he is faithful and just to forgive us our sins, and to cleanse us from all unrighteousness.*
>
> *– 1 John 1:9*

Here, the Bible says that if we confess our sins to God, He is faithful to forgive us and to cleanse us from all unrighteousness. In the matter of confession, we need to know two things. If we have sinned against God, we must confess our sins to God. If we have sinned against our fellow brothers or sisters, we must confess our sins to them and be reconciled with them. But how is the forgiveness materialized?

> *but if we walk in the light, as he is in the light, we have fellowship one with another, and the blood of Jesus Christ his Son cleanseth us from all sin.*
>
> *– 1 John 1:7*

From the above scripture, it is clear that we need to walk in the light to be forgiven of our sins. Walking in the light is to reconcile with God and with people by means of restitution. We should also have an intention to live right from that point forward. As we walk in the light, we will have fellowship with one another. Only then, the blood of Jesus will cleanse us from all sin.

COMMUNION WITH GOD

Then Jesus said unto them, Verily, verily, I say unto you, Except ye eat the flesh of the Son of man, and drink his blood, ye have no life in you.

– John 6:53

Always, it is the communion that establishes our relationship with God and our relationship with one another. It is intriguing to see that the word "Communion" means two different things here. The first is to partake in the flesh and blood of Jesus by means of the sanctified bread and wine. The second meaning of the word "Communion" is relationship. So, we can say that as we partake of the flesh and blood of Jesus, we establish our relationship with God.

Wherefore whosoever shall eat this bread, and drink this cup of the Lord, unworthily, shall be guilty of the body and blood of the Lord. But let a man examine himself, and so let him eat of that bread, and drink of that cup. For he that eateth and drinketh unworthily, eateth and drinketh damnation to himself, not discerning the Lord's body. For this cause many are weak and sickly among you, and many sleep.

– 1 Cor. 11:27-30

Is the practice of communion just a reminder of Jesus' sacrifice, or does it mean something more? As per the scripture above,

1. We are called not to partake of it unworthily. If we do, we will be guilty of desecrating the body and blood of Jesus.

2. We are called to examine ourselves. To examine is to repent of our sins before we partake of the communion.
3. If we partake unworthily, we will be damned.
4. We are called to discern that the communion is indeed the body of Christ.
5. When we do not discern, we will be weak and sick, and we may even die.

From the facts mentioned above, it is quite clear that communion is not just symbolic of the body and blood of Jesus; it is in fact the real body and blood of Jesus in the spiritual sense. Jesus indeed said that unless you eat my flesh and drink my blood, you have no part in the kingdom of God.

IMPLICATIONS OF SIN

When God created Adam, he was commanded to eat just the herbs and the vegetables. As Adam fell into sin, the entire human race became sinners. Cain murdered his brother, Abel. At the time of Noah, the sin was so excessive that God wiped out the whole earth by means of flooding. Noah was then asked to eat the animals. The sin of mankind was such that they even killed the prophets sent by God. Finally, they crucified Jesus himself, who is the only begotten Son of God. Man was now asked to eat the flesh and drink the blood of Jesus himself. This signifies the extent of mankind's sin.

GOD AS A GOOD FATHER

And ye have forgotten the exhortation which speaketh unto you as unto children,

My son, despise not thou the chastening of the Lord, Nor faint when thou art rebuked of him:

For whom the Lord loveth he chasteneth,

And scourgeth every son whom he receiveth.

If ye endure chastening, God dealeth with you as with sons; for what son is he whom the father chasteneth not? But if ye be without chastisement, whereof all are partakers, then are ye bastards, and not sons.

– Heb. 12:5-8

As we have made a covenant with God at the time of being born again, he always punishes us for our sins so we may learn not to do them again. We may think that this is a violation of our free will, but it is not. If we had not made a covenant with God, he would have left us alone to ourselves, but as we have entered into his covenant, he treats us as his children. We must understand that every good father corrects and disciplines his children.

CHAPTER 7

Perfection and Great Commission

A CALL TO FORSAKE OLD LIFESTYLE

This I say therefore, and testify in the Lord, that ye henceforth walk not as other Gentiles walk, in the vanity of their mind, having the understanding darkened, being alienated from the life of God through the ignorance that is in them, because of the blindness of their heart: who being past feeling have given themselves over unto lasciviousness, to work all uncleanness with greediness.

– Eph. 4:17-19

Most Christians tend to live an easy life not being serious about living a life of holiness. Here, the Bible commands us to forsake our old lifestyle and practice holiness.

PERFECTION, RIGHTEOUSNESS, AND HOLINESS

Therefore leaving the principles of the doctrine of Christ, let us go on unto perfection; not laying again the foundation of repentance from dead works, and of faith toward God, of the doctrine of baptisms, and of laying on of hands, and of resurrection of the dead, and of eternal judgment.

– Heb. 6:1, 2

The terms perfection, righteousness, and holiness: all mean the same thing. It is to stand right in the sight of God. As humans, we always tend to fall into temptation and sin. After we have fallen into sin, we regret our actions. We then repent of our sins and get right with God. A few days later, we are back in square one. We have fallen into sin again. If we keep encircling this lifestyle, God will never be able to use us. Since God has commissioned us with his great mandate to preach the gospel to every creature, how can we ever do this task if we ourselves are not able to rise up to that position? For this reason, the Bible mandates that we come to a stage of perfection. We may wonder how to achieve the perfection that God demands. We are perfected by our faith in Jesus Christ, which implies that we believe that the righteousness of Jesus is now imparted upon us as we allow him to live his life in and through us.

INHERITED RIGHTEOUSNESS

For what the law could not do, in that it was weak through the flesh, God sending his own Son in the likeness of sinful flesh, and for sin, condemned sin in the flesh: that the righteousness of the law might be fulfilled in us, who walk not after the flesh, but after the Spirit.

– Rom. 8:3, 4

Just as we had inherited the sin and curse of Adam, we have now inherited the righteousness of Jesus Christ as we place our faith in him, making sure to always walk in the spirit and not in the flesh. When we walk in the spirit, we are letting Jesus live his life through us, and we do not have a say of our own. It is a yielded and surrendered life.

PROGRESSIVE RIGHTEOUSNESS

For therein is the righteousness of God revealed from faith to faith:

as it is written, The just shall live by faith.

– Rom. 1:17

The scripture shown above says that we should live up to the perfection that God reveals to us as we grow from one level of faith to another. What it means is that God will not reveal all of the righteousness there is, but only to the level of our faith.

KNOWLEDGE-BASED RIGHTEOUSNESS

Therefore to him that knoweth to do good, and doeth it not, to him it is sin.

– Jam. 4:17

The scripture mentioned above says that we must do good to the level of our knowledge. There could be sins outside of our knowledge, but they are not accounted for. However, when it is brought to our knowledge, it becomes a sin. We must then repent of it and get right with God.

RIGHTEOUSNESS IN THE SPIRIT

For I say unto you, That except your righteousness shall exceed the righteousness of the scribes and Pharisees, ye shall in no case enter into the kingdom of heaven.

– Matt. 5:20

While we strive to remain perfect in the sight of God, we need to be careful not to work it out like the Pharisees. The Pharisees kept their prayer, fasting, and charity regularly, but with the wrong motive. They were anticipating praise from the people for their good work. In our case, we have already been saved, and we do not have to work out for our salvation. We only need to proclaim and declare our identity and position in Christ and confront every opposition that tells us otherwise. In other words, we must walk by faith and fight the good fight of faith to stay righteous in God's sight. If Satan has taken advantage of our weakness, we must wage spiritual warfare as well.

INDICATIONS OF RIGHTEOUSNESS

But the fruit of the Spirit is love, joy, peace, longsuffering, gentleness, goodness, faith, Meekness, temperance: against such there is no law.

– Gal. 5:22-23

How do we ever know if our salvation is taking effect in our lives in any way? When the fruit of the Spirit shows up in our lives, that is when we know that our salvation is taking effect in our lives. For example, if we were people of hate and intolerance and now we are loving and patient toward others, it means that we are being transformed. When the character of Christ is manifested in our lives, that is when we know that our salvation is taking effect in our lives.

I am crucified with Christ: nevertheless I live; yet not I, but Christ liveth in me: and the life which I now live in the flesh I live by the faith of the Son of God, who loved me, and gave himself for me.

– Gal. 2:20

The scripture shown above tells us that Paul was able to fully crucify his flesh because he says that he does not live anymore but that Christ lives through him. That is the state we need to arrive at if we are to be a blessing to others. We must strive to reach a point where none of the self will ever live, but Christ alone will take complete ownership of our lives. This is when our soul will be completely dominated by our spirit.

REACHING PERFECTION

Whosoever is born of God doth not commit sin; for his seed remaineth in him: and he cannot sin, because he is born of God.

– 1 John 3:9

The scripture above is quite bold to say that a person will not commit sin if he or she is born of God. However, 1 John 1:8 says, "*If we say that we have no sin, we deceive ourselves, and the truth is not in us."* So, how do we reconcile these two scriptures? According to Rom. 1:17, it says, *"For therein is the righteousness of God revealed from faith to faith: as it is written, The just shall live by faith."* Here, we understand that God will not reveal all of his righteousness outright. He reveals his righteousness to us progressively. If we remain faithful to the revealed righteousness, then 1 John 3:9 will be true. At the same time, there is a portion of unrighteousness in us which was not revealed to us by God. For this reason, 1 John 1:8 becomes true. Therefore, 1 John 3:9 and 1 John 1:8 both become true at all times. We will never be able to reach 100% of God's righteousness in this lifetime because 1 John 1:8 has to remain true at all times. Therefore, we can conclude that we can only reach perfection to the amount of righteousness that God has revealed to us.

In this scripture, the phrase, *"Whosoever is born of God"* also means *"Whosoever is the son of God"*. There are only two instances where a person becomes a "son of God". First, when the person receives Jesus Christ as his personal Lord and Savior. Second, when he walks in the spirit. Rom. 8:14 says, *"For as many as are led by the Spirit of God, they are the sons of God."* Only a person who is walking in the spirit can be led by the Spirit of God. Therefore, we can conclude that you are a "son of God" only when you walk in the spirt and when you are being led by the Spirit of God. So, we can rephrase the scripture 1 John 3:9 as *"Whosoever is the son of God doth not commit sin; for his seed remaineth in him: and he cannot sin, because he is born of God."* This verse cannot be applied to anyone else even if they are born again if they are walking in the flesh. We can also see this reiterated in Gal. 5:16 which says, *"This I say then, Walk in the Spirit, and ye shall not fulfil the lust of the flesh."*

From this, it is quite clear that when the Bible says in Mat. 5:48, *"Be ye therefore perfect, even as your Father which is in heaven is perfect."*, our perfection is only to the extent of God revealing his righteousness to us. If we are faithful in what has been revealed to us, then we are perfect.

THE GREAT COMMISSION

And he said unto them, Go ye into all the world, and preach the gospel to every creature. He that believeth and is baptized shall be saved; but he that believeth not shall be damned. And these signs shall follow them that believe; In my name shall they cast out devils; they shall speak with new tongues; They shall take up serpents; and if they drink any deadly thing, it shall not hurt them; they shall lay hands on the sick, and they shall recover.

– Mark 16:15-18

The purpose of our salvation is not just for us to be saved to go to heaven. It is also to share the same benefit to those who do not yet know Jesus Christ. As we go out into the world to share Christ, he has promised to be with us and demonstrate his power through our lives. As we share the gospel, we will be sharing more of what God has done in our own lives rather than sharing from what we have learnt about Christ. In other words, it is our testimonies that draw people to Christ and not our head-knowledge. While we yearn for our own perfection as we preach and teach others, it brings more glory to God and it also confirms the great work that God does in our lives by his grace.

CHAPTER 8

Condemnation and Judgment

REJECTING JESUS

He that believeth on him is not condemned: but he that believeth not is condemned already, because he hath not believed in the name of the only begotten Son of God. And this is the condemnation, that light is come into the world, and men loved darkness rather than light, because their deeds were evil. For every one that doeth evil hateth the light, neither cometh to the light, lest his deeds should be reproved. But he that doeth truth cometh to the light, that his deeds may be made manifest, that they are wrought in God.

– John 3:18-21

Condemnation begins in a person's life the moment he or she rejects Jesus as the Lord and Savior of their soul. Since God created us all, it is his sovereign right to invite us to him and tell us that he can save us and fix us. When we reject our creator, it is a rebellion of the highest sort.

TYPES OF SIN

If any man see his brother sin a sin which is not unto death, he shall ask, and he shall give him life for them that sin not unto death. There is a sin unto death: I do not say that he shall pray for it. All unrighteousness is sin: and there is a sin not unto death.

– 1 John 5:16, 17

The Bible says that there are two kinds of sin. One that leads to death, and one that does not lead to death. Here, the word "death" means to lose one's salvation. The fact that there is a sin that leads to death and we should not pray for it signifies that certain sins put a seal of condemnation on our lives that cannot be reversed.

But Peter said, Ananias, why has Satan filled your heart to lie to the Holy Ghost and to keep back part of the price of the land? While it remained, was it not thine own? and after it was sold, was it not in thine own power? why hast thou conceived this thing in thine heart? thou hast not lied unto men, but unto God. And Ananias hearing these words fell down, and gave up the ghost: and great fear came on all them that heard these things – Acts 5:3-5

The scripture shown above is an example of a sin that cannot be reversed. Ananias, who kept back part of the land price from offering it to the Lord, lied to Peter. But Peter says that he did not lie to him, but to the Holy Spirit. Ananias fell down dead even before he could repent.

> *Lest there be any fornicator, or profane person, as Esau, who, for one morsel of meat sold his birthright. For ye know how that afterward, when he would have inherited the blessing, he was rejected: for he found no place of repentance, though he sought it carefully with tears.*
>
> *– Heb. 12:16, 17*

The Bible gives another example of Esau, who lost his birthright and also his blessings, which he could never get even after he repented of them dearly.

CARELESS LIFE

> *Therefore we ought to give the more earnest heed to the things which we have heard, lest at any time we should let them slip. For if the word spoken by angels was stedfast, and every transgression*

and disobedience received a just recompence of reward; how shall
we escape, if we neglect so great salvation; which at the first began
to be spoken by the Lord, and was confirmed unto us by them that
heard him;

– Heb. 2:1-3

If we do not give much seriousness to the great gift of salvation we
have received, we will live a careless life, and we will not live up to the
expectations that God demands of us. When we exit the earth either by
death or by rapture, our salvation is decided by the state of our soul at
that time. If our soul is unrighteous, we will be condemned. If our soul
is righteous, we will be saved.

CONSEQUENCES OF IMPERFECTION

The Bible commands us to strive toward perfection so we may not miss
heaven. When we are perfect, we will not have to fear falling into sin.
Perfection is a condition where you always remain in the spirit and dare
not walk in the flesh. The consequences of imperfection can be seen in
the following verses:

For if we sin willfully after that we have received the knowledge of
the truth, there remaineth no more sacrifice for sins, but a certain
fearful looking for of judgment and fiery indignation, which
shall devour the adversaries. He that despised Moses' law died
without mercy under two or three witnesses: of how much sorer
punishment, suppose ye, shall he be thought worthy, who hath
trodden under foot the Son of God, and hath counted the blood of
the covenant, wherewith he was sanctified, an unholy thing, and
hath done despite unto the Spirit of grace?

– Heb. 10:26-29

When we fail to walk in the spirit, we fail to walk on the narrow road
that leads to eternal life. So, when we fall into sin, it is a sin because we
failed to walk in the spirit, either by negligence or by laziness.

For it is impossible for those who were once enlightened, and have tasted of the heavenly gift, and were made partakers of the Holy Ghost, and have tasted the good word of God, and the powers of the world to come, if they shall fall away, to renew them again unto repentance; seeing they crucify to themselves the Son of God afresh, and put him to an open shame.

– Heb. 6:4-6

Here, the Bible talks of sin that leads to death. In what instances do we think this can happen? It can only happen after we have tasted the power of God in our lives.

GOD's TERROR

For the time is come that judgment must begin at the house of God: and if it first begin at us, what shall the end be of them that obey not the gospel of God? And if the righteous scarcely be saved, where shall the ungodly and the sinner appear?

– 1 Pet. 4:17, 18

When we do not fear the Lord, we will have to face his terror. Before the great judgment day, God wants to filter his church and remove everyone who does not fear him and is not willing to live right.

For if after they have escaped the pollutions of the world through the knowledge of the Lord and Savior Jesus Christ, they are again entangled therein, and overcome, the latter end is worse with them than the beginning. For it had been better for them not to have known the way of righteousness, than, after they have known it, to turn from the holy commandment delivered unto them.

– 2 Pet. 2:20, 21

The scripture above clearly tells us that we are more accountable to God after having known him than if we had not known him.

CATEGORIES OF JUDGMENT

For as many as have sinned without law shall also perish without law: and as many as have sinned in the law shall be judged by the law; (for not the hearers of the law are just before God, but the doers of the law shall be justified.

– Rom. 2:12, 13

The scripture above speaks of two categories of people. People without law and people having the law. God expects that people without law may live by their conscience. Since the whole world is subjected to sin, people without law automatically perish. However, people who obey the law will be judged by the law based on their actions rather than their knowledge.

And to you who are troubled rest with us, when the Lord Jesus shall be revealed from heaven with his mighty angels, in flaming fire taking vengeance on them that know not God, and that obey not the gospel of our Lord Jesus Christ: who shall be punished with everlasting destruction from the presence of the Lord, and from the glory of his power;

– 2 Thes. 1:7-9

Here, the Bible says that when Jesus returns, he will take vengeance on two categories of people. First, those who do not know God. Second, those who did not obey the gospel.

JUDGMENT ON THE EARTH

And in them is fulfilled the prophecy of Esaias, which saith, By hearing ye shall hear, and shall not understand; And seeing ye shall see, and shall not perceive: For this people's heart is waxed gross, And their ears are dull of hearing, And their eyes they have closed; Lest at any time they should see with their eyes, And hear with their ears, And should understand with their heart, And should be converted, and I should heal them.

– Mat. 13:14-17

Even though we are living in the time of grace, there are certain sins that bring judgment while we are still here on earth. After Jesus had spoken the parable of the Sower, his disciples asked him why he spoke to them in parables. In reply, Jesus tells them that only those who seek to know the truth should understand. The rest of them should neither hear nor understand the things of God. This implies that people who care less about the things of God will be judged while they are still on earth. It will be hard for them to receive salvation, for they do not understand the things of God.

If any man see his brother sin a sin which is not unto death, he shall ask, and he shall give him life for them that sin not unto death. There is a sin unto death: I do not say that he shall pray for it. All unrighteousness is sin: and there is a sin not unto death.

– 1 John 5:16, 17

When God hardened the heart of Pharaoh, it was God's judgment on Pharaoh while he was still on earth. When Esau gave up his birthright, he could not receive blessings from his father Isaac later, which is kind of God's judgment on the earth. When Ananias and Sapphira fell dead while lying to Peter, it was God's judgment on the earth.

MISCONCEPTION ON PREDESTINATION

For this is good and acceptable in the sight of God our Savior; who will have all men to be saved, and to come unto the knowledge of the truth.

– 1 Tim. 2:3, 4

Some people believe that God has predestined some of the people to enter heaven and some of them not. They believe that the names of those who are predestined have been written in the Lamb's Book of Life and the names of those who have not been chosen is not written in the Lamb's Book of Life. This is a misconception and it is not true that God has selectively chosen some people to be saved and some to be damned. This heresy is derived from the scripture mentioned in Rom. 8:29 which says, *"For whom he did foreknow, he also did predestinate to be conformed to the image of his Son, that he might be the firstborn among many brethren."* Here, the scripture is not emphasizing on predestination. Instead, it is emphasizing on God's foreknowledge. It says that not everyone will be saved except those according to God's foreknowledge. The foreknowledge of God cannot be attributed to God as bad. But predestination would surely distort the integrity of God's love for mankind. Since God loves everyone, he desires that everyone should come into his kingdom and none should be lost. The Bible says that God has called many, but only a few have chosen to heed his call. Exo. 32:33 says, *"And the LORD said unto Moses, Whosoever hath sinned against me, him will I blot out of my book."* If predestination was true, why would God blot out the names of those who have committed sins, as their names should not have been written in the first place. In Rev. 3:5, Jesus reiterates this point and says, *"He that overcometh, the same shall be clothed in white raiment; and I will not blot out his name out of the book of life, but I will confess his name before my Father, and before his angels."*

CHAPTER 9

Father of Spirits

COMMUNICATION WITH OUR SPIRIT

Furthermore we have had fathers of our flesh which corrected us, and we gave them reverence: shall we not much rather be in subjection unto the Father of spirits, and live?

– Heb. 12:9

The verse shown above refers to God as the Father of spirits. That is because God always communicates with us in our spirit. When Adam was created, he was completely under the control of his spirit. In other words, he was being ruled by his spirit, which is the correct order. After he fell into sin, his spirit died, and then he was ruled by his body. As for us, once we are born again, we are placed in Adam's original place, where the spirit is able to rule our lives. However, it is at the discretion of our will whether to be ruled by our spirit or by our body.

Then shall the dust return to the earth as it was: and the spirit shall return unto God who gave it.

– Ecc. 12:7

The book of Ecclesiastes provides us with a clue as to what happens to our body and our spirit when we die.

WE ARE EVERYTHING THAT JESUS HIMSELF IS

But he that is joined unto the Lord is one spirit.

– 1 Cor. 6:17

When we are born again, the Spirit of God not only occupies our spirit, but we become one with Jesus in our spirit so that whatever Jesus is, we are the same.

For in him dwelleth all the fulness of the Godhead bodily. And ye are complete in him, which is the head of all principality and power: in whom also ye are circumcised with the circumcision made without hands, in putting off the body of the sins of the flesh by the circumcision of Christ: buried with him in baptism, wherein also ye are risen with him through the faith of the operation of God, who hath raised him from the dead.

– Col. 2:9-12

In Christ, we are completely made according to him. In him, we are circumcised, we are buried with him through baptism, and by faith, we are risen with him to live a holy and victorious life.

And if children, then heirs; heirs of God, and joint-heirs with Christ; if so be that we suffer with him, that we may be also glorified together.

– Rom. 8:17

Because of our union with Christ in our spirit, we become co-heirs with Christ, which means everything that Jesus has will also be ours.

SPIRITS IN PRISON

For Christ also hath once suffered for sins, the just for the unjust, that he might bring us to God, being put to death in the flesh, but quickened by the Spirit: by which also he went and preached unto the spirits in prison; which sometime were disobedient, when once the longsuffering of God waited in the days of Noah, while the ark was a preparing, wherein few, that is, eight souls were saved by water.

– 1 Pet. 3:18-20

And as it is appointed unto men once to die, but after this the judgment:

– Heb. 9:27

In the scriptures above, it says that the reason Jesus suffered on the cross was so that he could take us to God. It also says that Jesus, in his spirit form, went down to the prisons in hell and preached the gospel to the people who were disobedient in the days of Noah. It sounds like dead people may have another chance to be saved. But no, dead people do not have another chance to be saved. However, the people in the days of Noah are an exception.

For for this cause was the gospel preached also to them that are dead, that they might be judged according to men in the flesh, but live according to God in the spirit.

– 1 Pet. 4:6

When Jesus preached to the dead in prison, he judged them in their flesh but resurrected them in their spirit.

Wherefore, as by one man sin entered into the world, and death by sin; and so death passed upon all men, for that all have sinned: (for until the law sin was in the world: but sin is not imputed when there is no law. Nevertheless death reigned from Adam to Moses, even over them that had not sinned after the similitude of Adam's transgression, who is the figure of him that was to come.

– Rom. 5:12-14

The scripture above says that sin was present even before the law was introduced by Moses. When there is no law, sin should not be imputed upon the people. Since the people who lived in the days of Noah had no law, technically, they had not committed any sin. However, death reigned on them because of Adam's sin. For this reason, Jesus could go and preach to them, and that is why the exception.

SPIRIT WILL BE SAVED

For I verily, as absent in body, but present in spirit, have judged already, as though I were present, concerning him that hath so done this deed, in the name of our Lord Jesus Christ, when ye are gathered together, and my spirit, with the power of our Lord Jesus Christ, to deliver such an one unto Satan for the destruction of the flesh, that the spirit may be saved in the day of the Lord Jesus.

– 1 Cor. 5:5

Earlier, we saw that when Jesus preached to the spirits in prison, he judged them in the flesh, but they got saved in their spirit. Here is another instance where the person is judged in the flesh but whose spirit will be saved. This implies that the salvation of our spirit is permanent as long as we believe in Jesus. However, the soul will be saved as long as we walk by faith.

And fear not them which kill the body, but are not able to kill the soul: but rather fear him which is able to destroy both soul and body in hell.

– Mat. 10:28

In the scripture above, Jesus tells us not to fear those who can kill our body but cannot kill our soul. The reason they cannot kill our souls is because we are born again. As for those who want to kill us, Jesus says that their body and soul will be destroyed in hell. We need to make a note here that Jesus does not say what happens to the spirit. That is because their spirit will not be cast into hell but will be locked in a prison forever. But the spirit of those who are born again is already saved and will go to heaven.

And the very God of peace sanctify you wholly; and I pray God your whole spirit and soul and body be preserved blameless unto the coming of our Lord Jesus Christ.

– 1 Thes. 5:23

When Jesus returns, we need to be ready in the state of having been saved, not only in our spirit but also in our soul and body.

CHAPTER 10

The Final Victory

THE GREAT RAPTURE

Behold, I shew you a mystery; We shall not all sleep, but we shall all be changed, in a moment, in the twinkling of an eye, at the last trump: for the trumpet shall sound, and the dead shall be raised incorruptible, and we shall be changed. For this corruptible must put on incorruption, and this mortal must put on immortality. So when this corruptible shall have put on incorruption, and this mortal shall have put on immortality, then shall be brought to pass the saying that is written, Death is swallowed up in victory. O death, where is thy sting? O grave, where is thy victory? The sting of death is sin; and the strength of sin is the law. But thanks be to God, which giveth us the victory through our Lord Jesus Christ.

— 1 Cor. 15:51-57

The greatest victory that we will experience after having been saved is when we will overcome death and be lifted up to Jesus as he comes on the cloud to wage war against the anti-Christ and his minions.

For this we say unto you by the word of the Lord, that we which are alive and remain unto the coming of the Lord shall not prevent them which are asleep. For the Lord himself shall descend from heaven with a shout, with the voice of the archangel, and with the trump of God: and the dead in Christ shall rise first: then we which are alive and remain shall be caught up together with them in the clouds, to meet the Lord in the air: and so shall we ever be with the Lord.

– 1 Thes. 4:15-17

This amazing event is called the rapture. During the rapture, all those who are already dead and buried will rise first, and then those who are alive will be caught up with Jesus in the sky.

WAR IN THE HEAVENLIES

And there was war in heaven: Michael and his angels fought against the dragon; and the dragon fought and his angels, 8and prevailed not; neither was their place found any more in heaven. And the great dragon was cast out, that old serpent, called the Devil, and Satan, which deceiveth the whole world: he was cast out into the earth, and his angels were cast out with him. And I heard a loud voice saying in heaven, Now is come salvation, and strength, and the kingdom of our God, and the power of his Christ: for the accuser of our brethren is cast down, which accused them before our God day and night. And they overcame him by the blood of the Lamb, and by the word of their testimony; and they loved not their lives unto the death.

– Rev. 12:7-11

The rapture will not take place until a final war takes place between Archangel Michael and the devil. The initiators of this war are the people of God, known as saints, who will wage spiritual warfare. They will win this war by declaring the blood of Jesus and their testimonies, despite the threats they receive from leaders around the world. This will be the final battle that the saints of God will engage in before they are raptured.

THE CLIMAX OF SIN AND WICKEDNESS

For the mystery of iniquity doth already work: only he who now letteth will let, until he be taken out of the way. And then shall that Wicked be revealed, whom the Lord shall consume with the spirit of his mouth, and shall destroy with the brightness of his coming:

– 2 Thes. 2:7, 8

When the church allows sin and wickedness to go unchecked in this world, the time for the anti-Christ to be revealed to this world becomes closer and closer. The reason why sin and wickedness go unchecked is because Satan is targeting the saints not to focus on their mission by bringing worry, anxiety, and confusion into their lives.

PERSECUTION AND DEATHS

If the world hates you, ye know that it hated me before it hated you. If ye were of the world, the world would love his own: but because ye are not of the world, but I have chosen you out of the world, therefore the world hateth you. Remember the word that I said unto you, The servant is not greater than his lord. If they have persecuted me, they will also persecute you; if they have kept my saying, they will keep your's also. But all these things will they do unto you for my name's sake, because they know not him that sent me.

– John 15:18-21

The reason for the final battle begins with persecution. This world is being ruled by wickedness, while we are being ruled by righteousness. This is where the conflict is. The world will demand that we be their followers, but if we do, our salvation will be at stake. When we are persecuted, we must only remember that Jesus, our forerunner, was persecuted to the point of dying on the cross.

Fear none of those things which thou shalt suffer; behold, the devil shall cast some of you into prison, that ye may be tried; and ye shall have tribulation ten days: be thou faithful unto death, and I will give thee a crown of life.

– Rev. 2:10

As children of God, we will be put to the test in the last days. Jesus commands that we must remain faithful until the end, and we should not fear dying. Most of the apostles, like Paul, Peter, and Thomas, died as martyrs. John survived the persecution and wrote the book of Revelation, where Jesus revealed to him what would happen in the final days.

DEATH IS NOT OUR PORTION

And ye shall be hated of all men for my name's sake. But there shall not an hair of your head perish. In your patience possess ye your souls.

– Luke 21:17-19

Even though Jesus said that his people would die in persecution, death is not the perfect will of God. Jesus does not want any of us to die but to prevail over persecution and live.

He saith unto them, But whom say ye that I am?

And Simon Peter answered and said, Thou art the Christ, the Son of the living God. And Jesus answered and said unto him, Blessed art thou, Simon Bar-jona: for flesh and blood hath not revealed it unto thee, but my Father which is in heaven. And I say also unto thee, That thou art Peter, and upon this rock I will build my church; and the gates of hell shall not prevail against it. And I will give unto thee the keys of the kingdom of heaven: and whatsoever thou shalt bind on earth shall be bound in heaven: and whatsoever thou shalt loose on earth shall be loosed in heaven.

– Mat. 16:15-19

When Simon Peter declared Jesus as the Son of the Living God by means of the revelation knowledge from God, Jesus changed his name to Peter, which means rock. Then Jesus said that he would build his church on that rock. This implies that any church that is built on the revelation knowledge of the Word of God is the true church. To such a church, Jesus promises that the gates of hell shall not be able to prevail against it.

> *And from the days of John the Baptist until now, the kingdom of heaven suffereth violence, and the violent take it by force.*
>
> *– Mat. 11:12*

There will always be violence against the kingdom of God, but unless we have a violent attitude to fight against this violence, we will lose the kingdom.

> *When he had heard therefore that he was sick, he abode two days still in the same place where he was. Then after that saith he to his disciples, Let us go into Judæa again. His disciples say unto him, Master, the Jews of late sought to stone thee; and goest thou thither again? Jesus answered, Are there not twelve hours in the day? If any man walk in the day, he stumbleth not, because he seeth the light of this world. But if a man walk in the night, he stumbleth, because there is no light in him.*
>
> *– John 11:6-10*

When Jesus wanted to go to Lazarus tomb, the disciples warned him not to go. They said that there were Jews waiting to stone him. To this end, Jesus said that if anyone walks in the day, he will not stumble because there is sunlight and he will be able to see. But if anyone walks in the night, he will stumble because there is no light in him. Having no light in a person signifies not having the revelation knowledge of the Word of God. When you cannot grasp the Word of God as it was meant to be, you can be a victim of persecution.

There shall not any man be able to stand before thee all the days of thy life: as I was with Moses, so I will be with thee: I will not fail thee, nor forsake thee. Be strong and of a good courage: for unto this people shalt thou divide for an inheritance the land, which I sware unto their fathers to give them. Only be thou strong and very courageous, that thou mayest observe to do according to all the law, which Moses my servant commanded thee: turn not from it to the right hand or to the left, that thou mayest prosper whithersoever thou goest. This book of the law shall not depart out of thy mouth; but thou shalt meditate therein day and night, that thou mayest observe to do according to all that is written therein: for then thou shalt make thy way prosperous, and then thou shalt have good success. Have not I commanded thee? Be strong and of a good courage; be not afraid, neither be thou dismayed: for the Lord thy God is with thee whithersoever thou goest.

– Joshua 1:5-9

When Joshua took charge of leading the Israelites after Moses passed away, God assured Joshua that no one would be able to stand against him all the days of his life. God assures him by saying, "I will be with you; I will not fail you nor forsake you". God tells him repeatedly, "Be strong and of good courage; be not afraid, neither be thou dismayed". However, God gives him an instruction that will propel him to victory. The instruction is to observe the laws of Moses and not to turn from it to the right or to the left. The book of the law should not depart from his mouth. He should meditate on it day and night. It is then that Joshua will find himself succeeding in everything.

And ye shall be hated of all men for my name's sake. But there shall not an hair of your head perish. In your patience possess ye your souls.

– Luk. 21:17-19

In the New Testament, Jesus makes a similar statement to his disciples as he sends them two by two to all the villages of Israel to preach the gospel, to heal the sick, to deliver the oppressed, and to raise the dead. He warns his disciples that they will be hated by everyone, but not one of them shall be able to harm them, not even pluck one of their hairs.

Ye are of God, little children, and have overcome them: because greater is he that is in you, than he that is in the world. They are of the world: therefore speak they of the world, and the world heareth them. We are of God: he that knoweth God heareth us; he that is not of God heareth not us. Hereby know we the spirit of truth, and the spirit of error.

– 1 John 4:4-6

The reason we do not have to fear is because the Holy Spirit who is within us is greater than the spirits that are out in the world. When we preach the gospel to anyone, their response determines if they are from God or not. If they are not, we should leave them on their own.

POWER IN OUR WORDS

As the bird by wandering, as the swallow by flying, So the curse causeless shall not come.

– Pro. 26:2

The Bible says that no bad thing will ever happen unless there is a definite cause. If the perfect will of God for us is that we should not die during persecution, then we should know why God does allow death during persecution.

Death and life are in the power of the tongue:

And they that love it shall eat the fruit thereof.

– Pro. 18:21

The reason why people die prematurely is because of the negative words that they speak. Every negative word that we speak will bring a curse on our lives, which results in death.

> *And as we tarried there many days, there came down from Judæa a certain prophet, named Agabus. And when he was come unto us, he took Paul's girdle, and bound his own hands and feet, and said, Thus saith the Holy Ghost, So shall the Jews at Jerusalem bind the man that owneth this girdle, and shall deliver him into the hands of the Gentiles. And when we heard these things, both we, and they of that place, besought him not to go up to Jerusalem.*
>
> *Then Paul answered, What mean ye to weep and to break mine heart? for I am ready not to be bound only, but also to die at Jerusalem for the name of the Lord Jesus. And when he would not be persuaded, we ceased, saying, The will of the Lord be done.*
>
> *– Acts 21:10-14*

When the prophet Agabus warned Paul not to go to Jerusalem, Paul declared that he was willing not only to be bound but also to die for the name of the Lord Jesus.

> *And the Lord said, Simon, Simon, behold, Satan hath desired to have you, that he may sift you as wheat: but I have prayed for thee, that thy faith fail not: and when thou art converted, strengthen thy brethren. And he said unto him, Lord, I am ready to go with thee, both into prison, and to death.*
>
> *– Luke 22:31-33*

When Jesus informed Peter about the upcoming persecution in his life, Peter declared that he was ready to go to prison or even die.

> *Verily, verily, I say unto thee, When thou wast young, thou girdedst thyself, and walkedst whither thou wouldest: but when thou shalt be old, thou shalt stretch forth thy hands, and another shall gird thee, and carry thee whither thou wouldest not. This spake he,*

*signifying by what death he should glorify God. And when he had
spoken this, he saith unto him, Follow me.*

– John 21:18-19

As Peter had spoken of his willingness to go to prison or to die, Jesus
permitted him to die the death of a martyr.

*Then came to him the mother of Zebedee's children with her sons,
worshipping him, and desiring a certain thing of him. And he said
unto her, What wilt thou? She saith unto him, Grant that these
my two sons may sit, the one on thy right hand, and the other on
the left, in thy kingdom. But Jesus answered and said, Ye know
not what ye ask. Are ye able to drink of the cup that I shall drink
of, and to be baptized with the baptism that I am baptized with?
They say unto him, We are able. And he saith unto them, Ye shall
drink indeed of my cup, and be baptized with the baptism that
I am baptized with: but to sit on my right hand, and on my left,
is not mine to give, but it shall be given to them for whom it is
prepared of my Father.*

– Mat. 20:20-23

The mother of James and John, the sons of Zebedee, makes a request
to Jesus to have them seated next to him in his kingdom. Jesus asks her
if they are willing to be baptized with blood. Baptism in blood signifies
martyrdom, for which they say yes. As they said yes, Jesus assured
them that they would die the martyr's death. Moreover, Jesus says that
martyrdom is not the criterion for sitting next to Jesus in his kingdom.

*Then said Jesus unto them plainly, Lazarus is dead. And I am glad
for your sakes that I was not there, to the intent ye may believe;
nevertheless let us go unto him. Then said Thomas, which is called
Didymus, unto his fellow disciples, Let us also go, that we may die
with him.*

– John 11:14-16

When Jesus wanted to go to Lazarus' tomb, Thomas knew the kind of risk posed by Jesus. Thomas had said that there were Jews waiting to stone Jesus. Despite saying that, as Jesus was insisting that he would go, Thomas concedes to die with Jesus.

> *And they stoned Stephen, calling upon God, and saying, Lord Jesus, receive my spirit.*

> *– Acts 7:59*

We also see Stephen asking for death as the Jews were stoning him.

Postface

Now that you have completed reading this book, let us recap the message of salvation that changes your destiny forever. According to this salvation, you must remain blameless in your spirit, soul, and body when Jesus comes back the second time to this world.

> *And the very God of peace sanctify you wholly; and I pray God your whole spirit and soul and body be preserved blameless unto the coming of our Lord Jesus Christ.*
>
> *— 1 Thes. 5:23*

As per the Bible, God is a triune being. He exists as the Father, the Son, and the Holy Spirit. The Father legislates, the Son executes, and the Holy Spirit is the means by which it is executed. When God created man, he also created him as a triune being. Man is comprised of the spirit, soul, and body. The soul constitutes the real person while the spirit and body are just influencing factors over the soul. While the spirit influences the soul on godly matters, the body influences the soul on earthly matters. The spirit is God-conscious while the body is world-conscious.

When Adam and Eve, the first human beings, fell into sin, their spirits were disconnected from God. God cursed them and banished them from the Garden of Eden. For this reason, their spirit could no longer influence their soul on godly matters. They were now forced to be influenced by the five senses of their body, which are sight, sound, taste, smell, and touch. Every person who was born to them and to successive generations inherited the sin and curse of Adam. This caused mankind to degenerate in their moral behavior.

God, in his infinite wisdom, sent Jesus Christ, his Son into this world to represent mankind and pay the penalty of our sins by shedding his own blood. The mission was accomplished when Jesus Christ was crucified on the cross of Calvary. The shed blood of Jesus is the means by which our sins are forgiven as we repent of our sins and place our faith in his shed blood. By forgiving our sins, God is now inviting everyone to believe in the death and resurrection of Jesus Christ and to accept him as our personal Lord and Savior. By doing so, God wants to restore our spirit, which has lost its relationship with God. This paves the way for our salvation where we will receive the gift of eternal life and spend our eternity with God.

> *For the wages of sin is death, but the gift of God is eternal life through Jesus Christ our Lord.*

> *– 6:23*

> *Being justified freely by his grace through the redemption that is in Christ Jesus, Whom God hath set forth to be a propitiation through FAITH IN HIS BLOOD, to declare his righteousness for the remission of sins that are past, through the forbearance of God.*

> *– 3:24, 25*

> *that if thou shalt confess with thy mouth the Lord Jesus, and shalt believe in thine heart that God hath raised him from the dead, thou shalt be saved. For with the heart man believeth unto righteousness, and with the mouth confession is made unto salvation.*

> *– 10:9, 10*

Just as the spirit that had lost its relationship with God is now restored, similarly, the body that had inherited the sin and curse of Adam must be put to death. Unless the body that inherited the sin and curse of Adam is put to death, it is impossible for you to live a holy life because the curse of Adam will compel the body to commit sin against your will. This is done by means of water baptism. When you are water baptized, you identify yourself as having died with Christ, and you rise up as a new person. Your new nature is devoid of any sin or curse from

Adam. At this point, you are completely saved in your spirit, soul, and body.

> *Know ye not, that so many of us as were baptized into Jesus Christ were baptized into his death? knowing this, that our old man is crucified with him, that the body of sin might be destroyed, that henceforth we should not serve sin. For he that is dead is freed from sin.*
>
> *– Rom. 6:3, 6-7*

> *Therefore if any man be in Christ, he is a new creature: old things are passed away; behold, all things are become new.*
>
> *– 2 Cor. 5:17*

As a new person, you now have a new identity from God. As per this new identity,

1. You are a child of God.
2. You are adopted by God.
3. You are forgiven by God.
4. You are loved by God.
5. You are set apart for God.
6. You are the apple of God's eye.
7. God is fighting your spiritual battles.

As a new person, you have an inheritance as follows:

1. You are the righteousness of God.
2. You have the wisdom of God.
3. You have the mind of Christ.
4. You are a co-heir with Jesus Christ.
5. The Holy Spirit has taken his abode in you.
6. You no longer live, but Christ lives in and through you.
7. The grace of God is upon you.
8. All the promises of God will come true in your life.

As a new person, you have been given the following spiritual weapons:

1. The blood of Jesus
2. The name of Jesus
3. The Word of God

As a new person, your Christian Walk begins with faith and is sustained by faith. Faith is believing in your new identity, your new inheritance, and the spiritual weapons that are at your disposal. With this new mindset, you need to wage your spiritual warfare against every thought, word, or circumstance that works contrary to this new nature in you, using the spiritual weapons that have been given to you. If you ever fail to win this battle, you fall into sin once again, which defiles your soul and your body. By means of repentance and by partaking in communion, you get right with God and continue walking by faith again.

REVEALING GOD'S GLORY THROUGH OUR LIVES

As per your new nature, you need to manifest the following character through your life:

1. Love
2. Joy
3. Peace
4. Long-suffering
5. Gentleness
6. Goodness 7. Faith
7. Meekness
8. Self-control

This new nature is inherited in our spirit but is not yet manifested in our soul. This is manifested progressively as we wage spiritual warfare against the devil, who tries to oppress us, the agents of Satan that try to cast spells on us, and the untransformed part of our soul, which is called the flesh, that compels us to do things contrary to the new nature.

Every commandment of God must be kept by means of our new nature rather than trying to impose them against our will. Therefore, our utmost priority should be to get the new nature manifested in our lives rather than keeping the commandments of God. When the new nature is manifested, keeping the commandments of God becomes quite natural as part of our daily habits and not something we need to put in some sort of effort to keep.

Falling into sin in any area of our lives is an indicator that lets us know that the new nature in that particular area has still not been manifested in our lives. Falling into sin does not negate our salvation, but it is at stake. Our job in such a case is to repent of our sin, and work out the new nature in that particular area of our lives. Every time we conquer a particular area of our lives, we become a light to the world in that area of our lives.

This entire process of working out the new nature brings glory to God as the new nature is revealed to the world through our lives.

> *For we are his workmanship, created in Christ Jesus unto good works, which God hath before ordained that we should walk in them.*
>
> *– Eph. 2:10*
>
> *that we should be to the praise of his glory, who first trusted in Christ.*
>
> *– Eph. 1:12*

As long as we keep working out our new nature, our salvation is intact. If we ever become complacent and go back to this world and do not care to work out our new nature, our salvation is at stake.